FORENSIC INTERVIEWING OF A CRYPTID EYEWITNESS

Scott C. Marlowe

Cover by Peter Loh

First published in the United States by Pangea Press

Pangea Press
514 Winter Terrace
Winter Haven, FL
33881

ISBN: 978-1530489954

DEDICATION

For those who are engaged in the search and are truly interested in doing their research properly.

CONTENTS

INTRODUCTION

Every scientist knows that anecdotal evidence in cryptozoology is not sufficient proof that any cryptid creature actually exists in and of itself.

Human beings are so totally dependent on the five senses that we tend to forget how erroneous they can be. Our "reality" is actually compiled from the workings of different areas of our brain operating together and our perceptions are influenced by internal programming that tries to make sense of what we experience.

But essentially, the thing the human brain does best is to convince us that it works — that we are right about our perceptions.

In fact, this isn't so. Our brains fool us all the time. Thus, our perceptions of reality are not always as they seem or what we choose to believe they are.

Source: The Daily Omnivore

It is, for this reason, that accounts of cryptid sightings are not considered scientific proof of any creature's existence.

However, a researcher needs a starting place to begin investigating a sighting event in order to recover any physical evidence that may exist to support a creature's actuality and frequently that starting point must be anecdotal.

The problem with many such reports is that the investigator does not employ the proper technique for obtaining information about a sighting event. This failure almost always results in lost opportunities to discover actual evidence or worse, corrupts what evidence is actually recovered and calls the validity and reliability of that evidence into question.

Without first having interviewed an eyewitness, this "cryptid" animal track would never have been found and subsequent analysis would not have yielded a positive result.

The animal that made the track was later identified as a feral housecat and not the "Jaguarundi" that the eyewitness had claimed to have seen.

Photo Credit: Cal Allen

The purpose of this book then is to acquaint the investigator with proper forensic interviewing technique so that any information obtained from eyewitnesses to a cryptid sighting provides a solid, grounded basis for further research and the subsequent analysis of any physical evidence obtained during his or her investigations.

Pre-Interview Preparations

Preparing in advance of an interview will maximize the productiveness of eyewitness depositions and achieve greater efficiency in acquiring useful information about a cryptid sighting event.

Prior to performing an interview, the investigator should review any available information about the reported sighting event. This intelligence is likely to include but is not limited to, police reports, articles in periodicals, and weather reports. It is also a good idea to visit the site where the sighting occurred to familiarize yourself with "the lay of the land" so that you are able to visualize the events as described by the eyewitness in terms of the geographic features associated with the sighting event.

It is important that the research interviewer has as much relevant information about the sighting as possible before conducting the interview so that the meeting can be planned in advance and questions can be formulated to acquire the maximum amount of useful sighting data from the witness.

Since a cryptid sighting can cause traumatic stress in an eyewitness, the interviewer should arrange to conduct the interview as soon as the eyewitness is physically and emotionally able to communicate in a rational manner. Any undue delay in conducting the interview needs to be minimized to reduce the potential loss of detailed information since time tends to lessen an eyewitness' ability to recall material nuances of a sighting.

The interviewer should plan to conduct the interview in an

environment that minimizes distractions while maintaining the comfort level of the eyewitness. Distractions will hamper an eyewitness' recollection and chain of thought. So it is important to avoid interviewing an eyewitness in a location where distractions are likely to occur. Privacy is also desirable as many eyewitnesses fear ridicule by others when relating "weird" experiences.

Be sure than any mechanical resources you will be using during the interview are readily available (e.g., notepad, tape recorder, camcorder, interview room). Secure these items before the interview so the set-up of this equipment will not cause a distraction or interruption of the narration process. It is also important that your equipment is as unthreatening as possible.

If there is more than one eyewitness to a sighting event. it is essential to separate the witnesseses and meet with them separately.

Individual testimony can be used to reinforce and substantiate the deposition the other. Conversely, conflicting accounts will help you recognize the possibility that the report is not factual and staged or hoaxed for reasons you will have to determine.

Eyewitnesses should not be able to hear, or have access to, another witness' statement(s) since this can effect the statements provided by another eyewitness.

Try to discover as much personal background about an eyewitness as you can prior to making your first contact. This knowledge can help put any information obtained from the eyewitness into context for the purpose of assessing credibility and/or reliability. Moreover, knowing the eyewitness' background can become very helpful in developing a rapport with the eyewitness.

Preparing in advance for an eyewitness interview will enable the research investigator to obtain a greater quantity of useful and accurate information during an interview. Having valid and reliable data will become vital to the sighting investigation as research into the cryptid sighting event progresses.

Initial Contact with an Eyewitness

Research investigators should conduct themselves professionally and in a way that facilitates eliciting both quality information as well as quantity from an eyewitness.

Prior to beginning the interview, the person or persons who will be interviewing the eyewitness should try to develop a rapport with the interviewee. Gaining a rapport with the eyewitness will make 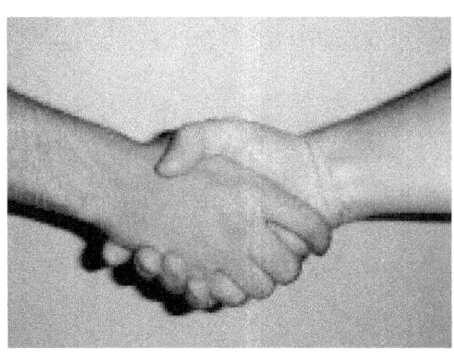 him or her more comfortable during the interview procedure. A comfortable eyewitness will usually provide a greater amount of information and will be more forthcoming. As the interviewer develops a rapport with the eyewitness the interviewer will also discern the witness' communication style. This is often revealing when analyzing eyewitness testimony. You should take note of how the eyewitness describes everyday events and compare this demeanor with how he or she describes the sighting incident.

However, you should avoid jumping to quick conclusions based on personality. For example, if the eyewitness appears nervous while developing a rapport with you, don't assume that this nervousness is a "red flag" that indicates the eyewitness' sighting account is a fabrication.

Inquire about the personality of a witness prior any contact related to the sighting. Prior contact related to the sighting could include conversations with law enforcement, media interviews, psychiatric sessions and so forth. Knowing about these encounters can help you put the eyewitness' account into proper context.

You should always ask the eyewitness if he or she has heard any other accounts of the sighting, been exposed to media coverage, or spoken to other eyewitnesses about the sighting event. This sort of communication is likely to "contaminate" the eyewitness' testimony.

Make a point of explaining to the eyewitness that your interview procedure involves contact related to witnessing the incident only. Do not ask the eyewitness about previous sightings that he or she may have had. You should have obtained this type of information during your preparation for the interview.

Do not volunteer specific information about the sighting event, your research or your thoughts regarding the incident to the eyewitness. Discussing facts or theories about the sighting may influence the eyewitness' memory of the incident and result in biased data. You must take appropriate care to ensure that any information you obtain from the eyewitness is based only on his or her memory and not on material gleaned from you or other sources.

By establishing a cooperative relationship with an eyewitness and conducting yourself professionally you will likely achieve an interview session that yields a larger quantity of quality information.

Conducting the Interview

There are four primary issues to consider when you conduct an interview with a cooperative eyewitness:

- The rapport between you (the interviewer) and the eyewitness.

- Facilitating the eyewitness's memory and reasoning ability.

- The Interaction between you (the interviewer) and the eyewitness.

- The continuity of the interview itself and interview process overall.

There are two main objectives crucial to setting up an opportune and viable social dynamic with an eyewitness.

Gaining foreknowledge about the eyewitness and his or her cryptid sighting event is just the beginning of establishing rapport. This information should help you gain some insight, and thus, empathy with the eyewitness. Empathy will go a long way in helping you achieve a productive interview relationship with the eyewitness.

When seeking to obtain information of a "bizarre" or confidential nature from anyone requires you to establish a personal relationship. Would you talk about sensitive or personal information with someone you didn't trust and respect?

Rapport development will help an eyewitness feel more at ease when conveying sensitive data. This can be accomplished by personalizing the interview. This is best accomplished by developing and communicating empathy. Demonstrating understanding and concern will help you develop a solid rapport with the eyewitness. Show compassion for the eyewitness' situation. Avoid judgmental comments and establish a common ground with the eyewitness.

As an interviewer, you should treat the eyewitness as an individual and not as a "statistic." Avoid scripted questions that sound programmed or artificial like: "Is there anything you can tell me that would further my investigation?" Always address the eyewitness by his or her proper name.

Endeavor to ask interactive questions that follow up on the eyewitness' previous responses whenever possible. Try to repeat an eyewitness' concerns in your inquiry and use effective body language that says, "I'm interested" — lean forward, and make eye contact.

Secondly, to be an effective interviewer, you need to encourage the eyewitness to respond actively and voluntarily with information about his or her sighting event. A passive eyewitness, one who responds only to the interviewer's questions, will not provide as much useful information as a dynamic eyewitness. Asking open-ended questions also allows the eyewitness to feel more in control. After all, that way they will do most of the talking during the interview.

Because the eyewitness, not the interviewer, possesses the relevant information about a sighting, the eyewitness needs to be mentally active during the interview. Stress can render a person lethargic and unresponsive. Allow the eyewitness to engage in behaviors that they will reduce their stress: walk around, drink (preferably decaffeinated) coffee or tea, look away while speaking, lower the lighting level, lie down, and so forth.

The interviewer can encourage the eyewitness to be mentally active by directly suggesting this kind activity or by asking open-ended questions. An open-ended question will allow for an unlimited, narrative response from the eyewitness. For example: "What can you tell me about your sighting?" is a better question than, "So, you saw a Big Foot at Pawley Creek?"

Avoid interrupting the eyewitness when he or she answers an open-ended question. You can also encourage an eyewitness to actively provide information by stating your expectations from the interview up front. This is important because an eyewitness is not likely to know what to expect, or may have false expectations, of his or her role in the interview. The interviewer should state explicitly at the beginning of the interview that the eyewitness is expected to volunteer information.

So, rather than interrupt a narrative, the interviewer should take notes and then follow up at a later time with any questions that may arise during the interview.

It is also important to allow pauses during the course of the interview. These pauses should occur after the eyewitness stops speaking about one issue and before he or she continues by answering the next question. These breaks in conversation will allow the eyewitness to gather his or her thoughts and continue responding with a clear picture of what they want to say. This frequently leads to a greater amount of detail information that is extremely useful in later research and field study.

By facilitating the eyewitness' memory and allowing time for he or she to think and recall events clearly, you'll get at detailed information about the sighting incident stored in the back recesses of eyewitness' mind. For the eyewitness to remember these events, he or she has to be able to concentrate and search through memory snippets efficiently.

Promoting Recollection and the Eyewitness's Memory

The interviewer can promote an eyewitness' memory and recall ability in several ways.

First, the interviewer should ensure that physical distraction like background noise and the proximity of other persons is limited or eliminated altogether. If distractions do occur during the interview, the interviewer can suggest that the eyewitness could block these distractions out by closing his or her eyes and concentrating only on their memory.

The interviewer can also help promote an eyewitness' expedient recollection of the sighting event by asking that the eyewitness mentally recreate the circumstances surrounding the incident in his or her "mind's eye." That is, the eyewitness should try to visualize his or her actions, and revisit thoughts or feelings just prior to, and at the time of, the sighting incident.

The interviewer should discern the aspect of the sighting the eyewitness is considering at that moment. Since the eyewitness is the central point of your interview, the interviewer should frame each question using the eyewitness' most current reflection and description.

For example, if the eyewitness is thinking or talking about a cryptid's appearance, your inquiry should stay on topic. Seek more detail about the creature's appearance. Do not raise questions about other aspects of the sighting until the current topic has been exhausted and the eyewitness wants to move ahead with another subject.

It is important for the interviewer to ask open-ended questions and then pursue clarification if needed. Ask follow up questions using non-leading, closed-ended inquiries connected to the point needing clarification. A closed-ended question is specific and framed in a way that limits the eyewitness' response to one or two words. For example, "How big was the animal you saw?"

When asking closed-ended questions, the interviewer needs to be sure that questions are not leading. A leading question proposes an answer to the eyewitness as well as an inquiry. "Was the animal's skin green?" is a leading question. "What did you observe about the animal's skin?" is not leading.

The interviewer has investigative needs to research an incident and the eyewitness possesses relevant knowledge about the details of a sighting. Both share a need to communicate effectively with each so that information obtained will contribute to a collection of facts that is useful in determining the true identity of the animal that is the focal point of the sighting event. Without verbal interchange, information critical to the investigation may not be completely or pragmatically covered.

The interviewer should explain the investigative requirements and clearly describe the general types of information required of the eyewitness. The investigator needs the eyewitness to discuss the sighting in far greater detail than would normally be conveyed in ordinary conversation. The investigator should be forthcoming about this need for detail to the eyewitness to ensure that the eyewitness understands the level of detail to include in his or her description.

Eyewitnesses frequently have very good memory of a

sighting but do not communicate their knowledge well. Therefore, the interviewer may need to facilitate the eyewitness' conversion of memory into effective speech. This can often be accomplished by encouraging nonverbal responses. Tell the eyewitness that he or she may draw illustrations, view pictures, and make hand gestures to supplement verbal descriptions if doing so would be helpful to them in offering their remarks.

The interviewer should also encourage the eyewitness to be candid about their statements and not edit his or her thoughts. The eyewitness should relate information as thoughts "pop into their head." But, the eyewitness should also be cautioned not to guess simply to satisfy the interviewer. Tell the eyewitness that you prefer that he or she say, "I don't know," or indicate uncertainty about an answer.

Sequencing the Interview

To be effective in obtaining the maximum amount of information from an eyewitness, the interview should be conducted in phases. The structure of the first phase of an interview is designed to relax the eyewitness and gain his or her confidence. In the next phase, the interviewer should provide general instructions – set the ground rules for the interview as discussed previously. The eyewitness' giving his or her narrative account of the sighting event should follow this. Finally, the interviewer should ask relevant, probing questions requesting clarification of points made by the eyewitness in his or her narrative that remain obscure or confused.

After this process is complete, the interviewer should then close the session while, leaving lines of communication open between the interviewer and eyewitness in the event that additional detail becomes necessary.

This is the "short and sweet" sequence for conducting an interview:

1. Attempt to minimize the eyewitness's anxiety.

2. Establish and maintain rapport with the eyewitness.

3. Encourage the eyewitness to take an active role in the interview.

4. Ask the eyewitness for an open narrative" ccount of the sighting.

5. Suggest that the eyewitness mentally recreate the

particulars of the sighting

6. Ask follow-up questions to obtain added detail related to the eyewitness' narration.

7. Review your notes and other materials for completeness and accuracy.

8. Ask the eyewitness, "Is there anything else I should have asked you?"

Closing an Interview

The researcher should endeavor to conduct a thorough, efficient, and effective interview of all eyewitnesses to a cryptid-sighting event and establish post-interview lines of communication between the eyewitnesses and the research interviewer.

Unprompted responses tend to provide more accurate detail than those answers given as a response to specific questions. The interviewer should use a structured format, like a fill-in-the-blank form, only after an interview session or sessions has collected as much information as possible from open-ended questions.

The eyewitness should be encouraged to talk about all the details of a sighting event even if some details seem to be trivial or unimportant. Relevant information is often withheld because an eyewitness thinks some detail is unimportant or is out of chronological order. The interviewer should assure the eyewitness that information he or she possesses could turn out to be extremely important.

Ask the eyewitness to contact you (the investigator) when and if additional information is recalled. Eyewitnesses will often remember additional useful information after an interview session. Remind the eyewitness that information that seems unimportant may turn out to be vital to the sighting investigation.

The interviewer should ask the eyewitness to avoid discussing details of the sighting with other eyewitnesses. Eyewitnesses should not be privy to other accounts because hearing about them may influence or cloud the eyewitness' recollection of events. The independence of eyewitnesses is material to the corroboration of the information the eyewitness provides and the amalgamation of statements from all eyewitnesses becomes compelling testimony to a sighting and significant evidence in the investigation of a cryptid encounter.

The eyewitness should also avoid media contact or exposure to media renditions concerning the sighting. Media articles are frequently inaccurate and can adulterate the eyewitness' recollection of events and details concerning a sighting. Media requests for an interview or offers of compensation can also invite the eyewitnesses to fabricate information.

The interviewer should thank the eyewitness for his or her collaboration. Doing so will reinforce the rapport that has been developed and the interviewer's commitment to the eyewitness, encouraging the eyewitness to continue his or her cooperation.

Recording Witness Recollections

A tape recording of eyewitness sighting accounts accurately and thoroughly records all information obtained and preserves the integrity of oral evidence. But, if a tape recorder isn't available or isn't practical the investigator should make a complete and accurate written record of all information obtained from eyewitnesses.

This written report should be made during the eyewitness interview or, if this isn't possible, as soon as practical and reasonable after the interview.

Regardless of the documentation format chosen (tape recording, video, stenographer, court reporter, et cetera) the report should include the eyewitness's narrative account of the sighting, a written summary of the events using, wherever possible, the witness's own words, drawings, illustrations, photographs, ID charts and copies of all written materials germane to the investigation.

This documentation is imperative should the eyewitness become unavailable later in the investigation. Use of the witness' own language and written material ensures that the research data is recorded accurately. It is also a good idea to have the eyewitness attest to the accuracy of information provide by signing off on the report.

Make a follow-up appointment with the eyewitness to review all the documentation to assure accuracy and completeness. Be sure to ask the eyewitness at that time if there is anything he or she would like to change, add, or expand upon. This gives you another opportunity to clarify information provided by the eyewitness to assure all information has been recorded properly.

Complete and accurate documentation of eyewitness statements become the successful foundation for further investigation and any future research and field study.

Although sometimes necessary, the additional personnel and video recording equipment may be quite intimidating to an eyewitness. So much so that it becomes counter-productive. Consider, where ever possible, using a small recording device like a palm-size digital recorder instead.

Assessing the Accuracy of Individual Elements of an Eyewitness Statement

These assessment procedures should be conducted after the actual interview and without the eyewitness present.

Consider each point of an eyewitness' statement individually to judge the details of the statement that are most likely accurate. Each piece of information recalled by the eyewitness could be remembered independent of other elements or out of sequence.

An eyewitness may not have complete information about all elements of a sighting. Therefore, some individual recollections may be correct while others may not.

Review each element of the eyewitness' statement in the context of the entire statement. Look for inconsistencies within the overall statement. Note these inconsistencies for future reference. Also, note that an inconsistency in one element of the statement does not mean that the entire statement is inaccurate.

Be sure to review each part of the eyewitness' statement in the context of the evidence from other sources (e.g., other eyewitness statements, physical evidence, historical and previous sightings).Note any inconsistencies between the eyewitness' statement and other information. These inconsistencies can be useful in assessing the accuracy of different points or aspects of eyewitness statements as well as in directing the investigation.

Following this technique will avoid the common misconception that the accuracy of an individual element of an eyewitness's description predicts the accuracy of another element and often results in a more complete description of events when all forms of evidence are taken into account.

Maintaining Contact With An Eyewitness

Eyewitness' can often remember and provide additional detail after the physical interview has been concluded. The investigator should maintain open communication to allow the eyewitness to provide any additional information.

During post-interview follow-up the investigator should contact with the eyewitness. Begin each contact by reestablishing rapport with the eyewitness. The investigator should ask the eyewitness about something personal that follows up on his/her previous contact with the eyewitness. Eyewitnesses will feel comfortable providing information to investigators with whom they have a continuous positive relationship.

Ask the eyewitness if he/she has recalled any additional information. This reinforces the idea that the eyewitness is an active part of the investigation.

Be sure to follow the interviewing and documentation procedures we have previously covered in all post-interview communication with an eyewitness.

Eyewitness Contamination and Follow-up Contact

Instruct your eyewitness to direct any requests from other investigators for interviews to you. Provide no information from other sources to your eyewitnesses and insist on being present during any interrogation of an eyewitness by other researchers, media or investigator during an active investigation.

Obtain credentials from any person requesting contact with your eyewitness. Check out their credentials thoroughly to be sure that unqualified persons do not make contact with your eyewitness as there is a danger that this contact would alter (contaminate) the eyewitness' recollection of events.

You should require a list of written questions from these interrogators to review prior to their interview. Refuse questions that are leading, improperly phrased, threatening, hypothetical or philosophical in nature.

Eyewitnesses often ask the investigator about information that has developed since the initial interview. Providing the eyewitness with specific information obtained from other eyewitnesses, or from physical evidence, may also influence the eyewitness' perception of the incident. You should politely avoid providing this information by saying that the investigation is on-going and it is too soon to discuss the evidence until it can be properly verified.

Should other information arise following the initial interview that differs from, contradicts, or corroborates information the eyewitness provided, this information can be clarified with the eyewitness in follow-up interviews or casual contact. However, the investigator should present clarifying questions to the eyewitness in a non-leading manner. The investigator should ask additional questions of the eyewitness with neutral information, such as asking, *"was any other person present at the time of the sighting,"* NOT *"Are you sure that Joe Blow wasn't at the scene?"*

Reestablishing contact and maintaining a rapport with an eyewitness often leads to recovery of additional information later in your investigation. Maintaining open communication channels with the eyewitness throughout the investigation can also lead to additional physical evidence.

Meet the Author:
Scott Marlowe

Proclaimed as, "America's most credible cryptozoologist," Scott Marlowe, spends as much time in camos and boots as he does in a lab coat and oxfords.

A Fellow Of the famed Pangea Institute and educational consultant to the American Primate Conservation Alliance, Marlowe is the first expert in the field to succeed in establishing an on-going college level course in cryptozoology at a state institution of higher learning anywhere in the world.

His cryptozoology course, hailed as one of the "Top Ten" news stories of 2004 by The Cryptozoologist, a well-known insider eMagazine, has won both accolades and awards for its fresh approach and application of forensic science methodologies to the study enigmatic animals.

Marlowe's television credits include, MonsterQuest, Is it True, Legend Hunters, Destination Truth, Weird Travels, and Silliam Shatner's Weird or What? in addition to countless radio appearances, TV guest spots and lecture tours.

www.ingramcontent.com/pod-product-compliance
Lightning Source LLC
Chambersburg PA
CBHW071317280526
45788CB00004B/1921